Book Lovers

Sharing the Pleasure of Reading

Book

Sharing the

INTERVIEWS & PHOTOGRAPHS BY *Susan Rogers*

Pleasure of Reading

Lovers

Grass Roots Press

Edmonton, Alberta, Canada
2005

Book Lovers is published by

Grass Roots Press
A division of Literacy Services of Canada ltd.
P.O. Box 52192, Edmonton, Alberta, T6G 2T5, Canada
Phone: 1-780-413-6491
Fax: 1-780-413-6582
Web: www.literacyservices.com

Author: Susan Rogers
Photographer: Susan Rogers
Book Design: Lara Minja, Lime Design Inc.
Editor: Anne Le Rougetel
Printing: Friesens, Manitoba

We acknowledge the financial support of the Government of Canada
through the Book Publishing Industry Development Program (BPIDP)
for our publishing activities.

We acknowledge the support of the Alberta Foundation for the Arts
for our publishing program.

Library and Archives Canada Cataloguing in Publication

Rogers, Susan, 1952-
    Book lovers / Susan Rogers.

    ISBN 1-894593-34-0
    1. Books and reading. 2. Reading interests. I. Title.
Z1003.R63 2005   028'.9'0971   C2004-905536-4

Printed in Canada

To

my family who love

reading as much as I do.

— Susan Rogers

Table of Contents

Introduction
PAGE 8

Reading

enriches our lives by broadening our knowledge of life and helping us to understand and empathize with other people. Reading is also the ideal way to carve out private time for ourselves within our homes. ✤

Introduction

"HAS ANYONE SEEN THE LEMON BOOK?" called out my husband. I gathered he was speaking to me as I am the finder of all things in our household. It was actually the second time I'd been asked that question in the space of a couple of hours. That's because everyone in our household was reading *Driving Over Lemons*[1] simultaneously. I had instigated this little tug of war by urging them to read the book because it's both very funny and very informative.

Knowing that my family enjoyed the book as much as I did doubled my pleasure and gave us great dinner conversation as we recalled our favourite bits. When I chatted to the readers interviewed for this book, I found out that wanting to share your pleasure over a great read is almost universal among book lovers. Perhaps it's because sharing stories takes reading from a solitary experience to a social one.

While it's common to talk about books, it's less common to discuss reading itself. The idea for this book sprang from a curiosity about why people read, what they read, and how they read. This book's collection of excerpts from conversations is an opportunity to share some of the things that people told me about reading. I interviewed thirty individuals and four reading groups so that I could explore both the private and the social aspects of reading.

Reading doesn't get much attention as a hobby. Few books are written about it compared to, say, fishing, meditation, golf, cooking, or any of the many other activities we do for pleasure. Yet I suspect it's one of the most common hobbies people list on their resumés. It could be that reading doesn't attract much attention because people tend to read when they are alone or in a private setting, so the act of reading is often unseen. Perhaps reading is too commonplace. People who learnt to read as children often take the ability to read for granted. In that respect reading is like a beloved friend, a companion that is always with you and completely amenable to your needs. So it's time to shine a spotlight on this old pal and take a look at reading from the perspective of book lovers. >

I DISCOVERED THAT READERS HAVE VERY INDIVIDUAL APPROACHES TO READING. Yet certain themes recurred in our conversations. Reading is relaxing and it helps us make a transition from work to rest or vice a versa. That may be why many of us like to read in the evening or first thing in the morning.

Reading is also solace—when things go wrong, reading allows us to escape and forget about our immediate problems. But perhaps the most common theme is that readers relish the way books enable them to explore different lives, whether in known territory or in exotic settings. Reading enriches our lives by broadening our knowledge of life and helping us to understand and empathize with other people. Reading is also the ideal way to carve out private time for ourselves within our homes.

When I don't have anything to read I feel slightly frantic. I can usually ensure that this doesn't happen at home but it's common enough when travelling. In hotel rooms, I'll quite happily read tourist information, old magazines, or even *The Yellow Pages*, just to satisfy the need to read. Of course, it's impossible to separate reading from a discussion of what we read, and avid readers don't just read books—despite the title of this book. But *Book Lovers* does seem to encapsulate the essence of what reading is all about. Yes, people read and enjoy the Internet, magazines, newspapers, comics, telephone directories, and numerous other bits of information, but books are what satisfy most of us, most of the time.

Readers like to talk about books and love to share their great finds. But when it comes to a choice of fiction or nonfiction, it was clear that most of the people I met preferred fiction. I had an inkling that this would be so because whenever I've wanted to join a book club, I've always been disappointed that other members didn't show much enthusiasm for nonfiction. This has never bothered me because—apart from not being able to join book groups—I have, until this point, been quite happy with my reading choices. However, during my conversations with readers, I began to reconsider my reluctance to pick up fiction. Hearing readers enthuse about what certain books of fiction have meant to them made me want to read those books as well. With each interview, you'll find a list of the books they were enthusiastic about. It's my current reading list. (For lovers of nonfiction there are some of those as well.)

We often don't have clear memories of how we actually learnt to read, although the people I interviewed had fond memories of reading as children and had no problem recalling the plots of well loved books. I, too, remember my early readers and the way the simple sentences looked on the page. 'See Dick run. See Jane run.' Those early narratives bored me, but then suddenly it seemed I could

Yes, people read and enjoy the Internet, magazines, newspapers, comics, telephone directories, and numerous other bits of information, but books are what satisfy most of us, most of the time.

read anything I wanted and I was swept away by the excitement of children's adventure stories. One day in the library I remember looking at shelves of adult books and worrying about getting older and having to read these dull looking books. Little did I know that some worries are groundless.

The first thing I do when I move to a new place is to join the library and I'm not alone in this respect. But readers also like to own books and love to hang around bookstores. It's comforting to be surrounded by books whether in a library, bookstore, or at home. Book lovers always struggle with what to do with the books they own. Most collectors can't bear to be parted from their old friends but eventually a move or cleanout necessitates a trip to the second hand bookstore or charity shop. Nobody ever throws books in the garbage.

Readers are also divided on how to treat books. Some people wouldn't dream of marking a book, while others happily underline important points or make notes to themselves. I heard about one woman who tore strips off the cover to use as a bookmark. This made me shudder. I'm firmly on the side of those who keep their books in pristine condition—unlike my son who bends spines, drops books in the bath, stuffs them in bags, and generally mistreats them.

Many people mentioned how much they love the smell of old books and the feel of leather-bound books and crisp white pages. Yet just as many people prefer paperbacks because they are light and easy to hold.

One of the joys of reading is that it is a portable hobby—unless you like to read on a computer, which doesn't seem to be common among the people I interviewed. They take their books on buses, trains, boats, and planes. They read while waiting, exercising, or even walking. But it's clear that there are favourite places to read. The bath is definitely high on the list, in spite of the hazard of water to a book. Our beds are another popular place, although many people mentioned that it's too easy to lose out on sleep. Reading and eating at the table is also very popular although some people stressed that they only do it when they're alone. I don't, but fortunately my husband shares this little vice. Some people like to read in coffee shops but others find the hustle too distracting. The beach is a classic location, but surprisingly no one mentioned reading while sitting on the toilet. Perhaps they didn't want to risk a photograph in that compromising position!

After talking to so many people I have no doubt that reading is a subject that inspires passion and enthusiasm. Our conversations were stimulating and it was hard to know when to end the discussion, but time pressures and the thought of transcribing hours of tape eventually brought things to a conclusion. Thank you all, for sharing your thoughts about reading and books with me and a special thank you to Pat Campbell for coming up with the idea for this book and collaborating with me.

In the end, I think, we can all agree with Nuala O'Faolain, who wrote, "If there was nothing else, reading would—obviously—be worth living for."[2] 🦉

Some people wouldn't dream of marking a book, while others happily underline important points or make notes to themselves.

Notes

1. Stewart, C. (2000). *Driving over lemons: An optimist in Andalucia.* NY: Pantheon.

2. O'Faolain, N. (1998). *Are you somebody?: The accidental memoir of a Dublin woman.* NY: Henry Holt.

"When you read a story it's like diving in, and then you resurface later and you never resurface the same person as you were before." ✳

Reading List

Blindness - Jose Saramago

Punished by Rewards: The Trouble with Gold Stars, Incentive Plans, A's, Praise, and Other Rewards - Alfie Kohn

Hegemony or Survival: America's Quest for Global Dominance - Noam Chomsky

RITA IS AN AWARD-WINNING WRITER FROM BRAZIL. She immigrated to Canada three years ago and admits that it is a challenge to write in English but she is happy to live here. Her first poem in English was recently published in a literary journal.

"I've always had a relationship with reading that is very non-judgmental. Right now I'm reading in a very different way. I don't think it'll be forever, but I'm new here so I have to learn a different language. Here there are very different parameters about how to write, so I started reading books and looking for those elements. I read them now as if I were a doctor opening a body—and sometimes it can be ugly. But it's very interesting because I started paying attention to description, setting and characters. It's a different type of enjoyment—an intellectual enjoyment.

Reading poetry for me is a lot like hearing music. It's something you can read over and over again like you can listen to the same song and you never get tired of it. But reading fiction is more like watching a movie. You can do it again but there is no surprise.

When you read a story it's like diving in, and then you resurface later and you never resurface the same person as you were before. That's the function of good literature for me—to change you in some way whether because you lived someone else's life so you learn to empathize or because you saw yourself better during this travel.

I can't imagine a child not reading if you yourself are a reader. But it's more than setting an example. Although reading looks like an individual thing to do, it's very social. In my family we talk about the books together. Sometimes we find a funny bit and say, 'Listen to this.' These are interactions so that if you are a household of readers you're talking about books and sharing stuff all the time.

It's interesting that when we say reading we always think of reading books, but when you're hearing a story you're reading spoken words—it's the same thing. The storytelling movement is really strong in Canada and I've enjoyed that. It's a more collective way of reading.

Everything that is important to you, you like to share. I have so many fulfilling experiences related to reading and I just want people to feel the same and go through the same pleasure. When you read the same book you feel like the person is living the same thing you did.

When they started publishing books and newspapers someone would read the chapters for the whole family. This experience is an important dimension of reading—we can't throw this away." ❧

"When you read a story it's like diving in, and then you resurface later and you never resurface the same person as you were before."

TOLOLWA IS AN ARUSHA MAASAI WHO GREW UP IN TANZANIA. He has lived in Edmonton for sixteen years. He grew up hearing stories and now makes use of African folktales in his published work. He's currently finishing up a doctorate in English and drama.

"I grew up in a very small place. I had no books at home. The school only had two grades and two teachers. One of them was my father. Nobody would have imagined anyone having books at home except maybe the Bible. You only got your first book when you started school and that was a little complicated because they looked at how big you were not how old. A lot of kids had no records. So my friends started school before I did. They got to learn to read and I thought it was absolutely magic the fact that they could pick out these things written on the board.

I became fascinated with books. I got my first book and it was so special. It was just an alphabet reading book. After that I started reading everything I could lay my hands on—things bought from the store, even things in English, but I didn't speak English. I read it in a Swahili kind of way. I didn't know what I was saying. It just sounded neat.

I didn't get any extra books until I went to this boarding school in Grade 6. My uncle was the principal of the school and he just loved books, so there were books from everywhere including the States. And I read all of them—there weren't that many—including encyclopedias. We'd start from 'A' as if you were reading a novel. I read a lot of English folk tales. Everything that you really love, you start writing in the style of that. So I started writing this long story imagining myself being this knight in a castle close to the river Thames. I went on and on— I must have written over a hundred pages before I went on to something else.

In the secondary school we had a musty library, which was only open twice a week—Tuesday and Thursday afternoon. I lived for those days. I'd make sure on Tuesday that I chose a small book (you could only borrow one book at a time) that I could finish by Thursday, and then on Thursday I'd make sure I got a bigger book. One time I got *The Three Musketeers*. I loved it but I had to finish it by Tuesday and I forgot to do my homework. I was the first one to be picked to read my story and I hadn't written anything. I made up the story and I surprised myself but then the teacher said, 'Can I have your notebook?' He looked at it and said, 'I was able to tell that you'd not written it because your eyes were not moving.'" ❦

"Nobody would have imagined anyone having books at home except maybe the Bible."

"When I was a child, my reading experience was something very close to my heart."

"I love writers who can make me laugh when I read." ✤

Reading List

The Curious Incident of the Dog in the Night-Time - Mark Haddon

Bridget Jones's Diary - Helen Fielding

Inside Mr. Enderby - Anthony Burgess

The Oxford Dictionary of Humourous Quotations - Ned Sherrin

Val Somerville

VAL DESCRIBES HERSELF AS A CROSSWORD ADDICT, a lover of bookstores, and an avid reader of the New York Times Book Review. She grew up in the north of England and later travelled the world as an air hostess before settling down in Vancouver.

"When I discovered the library I was fascinated. I made the books I owned into library books. There used to be a pocket inside with a card that would get stamped. I would loan them to my little friends.

I loved the library but I used to get into trouble because I forgot to take books back and the fines would be horrendous. I didn't have any money and my mum would get mad. She sometimes tore up my library card but she always let me get another one eventually.

I've never forgotten one book called *The Tree that Sat Down* by Beverley Nichols. A girl and her grandmother lived in the hollow of an old tree in the forest with all the creatures of the forest. There was an owl who was the judge for any disputes. I remember he'd say (he must have seen American movies), 'S'helpmegod,' because he didn't want to swear. And there was a witch, but she was a thoroughly modern witch—she rode a motorcycle and she had flaming hair and when she got off the motorcycle her wig came off and her teeth came out.

I'm sure it's long out of print—I think I gave my copy to one of my nephews so it's somewhere in the family. I'd like to try and find it. We're talking 60 years ago and I remember it so well. I loved it.

I think I imagined being the little girl. We lived in a block of flats in the centre of an industrial city—no forests. They were stuff of magic to me. It was the same when I read Enid Blyton or Arthur Ransome's descriptions of characters messing about in boats—it was hard for me to believe that children lived lives like that. I did transport myself to that setting. And the little girl was safe because all these creatures were friendly.

It was the blackout. I was a little girl during the war. It was frightening in the darkness so these books reassured me. Later, when I met kids whose parents had a car and went to the lakes to go in a boat, I couldn't believe it. I thought it was just the stuff of books." 🍎

"It was frightening in the darkness so these books reassured me."

Sean Boomer

SEAN AGREES THAT BOOKS PLAY A MAJOR ROLE IN HIS LIFE. "Since I've been an adult, I've been a student or a researcher and now I work in a bookstore and one of my main pastimes is reading." Sean grew up in Ontario. He describes his parents as working class Irish and he credits his dad with first introducing him to books and history.

"Two books that had a profound impact on me were, *I Claudius* and *Claudius the God* by Robert Graves. I found those books quite fascinating and they also helped develop an interest in ancient Rome which became quite important in my studies later on.

The main character, Claudius, suffered from some of the things that I had suffered from growing up, and in a sense still suffer from. Up until I was fourteen, I had a stutter, and Claudius, of course, has a stutter. I've always had bad coordination, so much so that I was often taken aside for extra classes on handwriting and what not. And Claudius has trouble functioning as an adult in society.

"It heightened for me the importance of my view of the world and my understanding of life, as opposed to accepting other people's judgments."

Even now the whole issue of being an outsider and not being able to do everything that everyone else can do, and to some extent being looked down on because of that, really resonates with me. Reading those books made me feel better. I certainly identified with the main character. It made me sad as well because in the end even though Claudius has integrated with society and achieved something valuable he has been lied to by others. But it reminded me that even if other people view you as being less than they are that doesn't mean that you are.

It heightened for me the importance of my view of the world and my understanding of life, as opposed to accepting other people's judgments. The whole point of the novel is that Claudius is very intelligent and is able to see things that other people don't see. That was an extremely valuable insight and it did make me feel better. Although it's more than that. It's what the Greeks would call catharsis, which is suffering with someone else and going through their sense of tragedy and the feeling of being purified at the end—and I did get that out of *I Claudius*. I don't know if that was the intent of Robert Graves when he wrote it but it certainly moved me." ❦

"I'm a slow reader. I don't skim through books, I tend to read very thoroughly."

"I read to keep
my mind still,
to fill it when
it's empty." ❖

Patricia Murphy

PATRICIA, A.K.A MURPH, likes to celebrate her Irish heritage by throwing a great

St. Patrick's Day party in her cooperative housing building in Vancouver. She admits that reading

is often an escape for her, as she suffers periodically from depression.

"I started reading mysteries on a regular basis when I was going into depression. I tried to figure out why I got so into mysteries. In depression I have a hard time feeling anything and I think I needed to read something that was violent. I like scary books. I kinda need shaking up—my life is pretty blah. I also like the comfortable mystery stories but not as much.

I feel for the detective. If I don't like the detective I won't like the mystery. Also, I read the end first because I get too anxious—it's not finding out who did it, it's finding out how the detective finds out. It's like cheating at a game, but I'm playing this game by myself—so I find it really healthy to do that. Also I get impatient and I can't enjoy all the details of the book.

I prefer to own books. I'd own a lot more if I had the money. Books are the things I most prefer to buy. When I did have money that's what I bought. But books are very expensive and I have a hard time holding hardcover books so I wait until they come out in soft cover. There's a great bookstore right beside my bank which is unfortunate. *(Laughs.)*

"I prefer to own books. I'd own a lot more if I had the money. Books are the things I most prefer to buy."

I entered a religious order and for three and a half years I didn't read anything except pious books, which weren't very interesting. You couldn't read anything without permission. So when I went to university and had access to the libraries I was in heaven. I stayed in the religious order for fifteen years. Later on things eased off and I could read.

Since October [last year] I haven't had access to my books. They've been packed in boxes because of repairs in the apartment. It's been terrible not to be able to find things in my books. I watched the film *Mystic River* and I wanted to read the book again but I couldn't find it. It was awful. I finally just about threw a tantrum and said, I have to have my books out. I like to have the books well organized—it's real manic but I get satisfaction from it and it's easier to find things." 🍎

R AJ WAS BORN IN PUNJAB, INDIA AND HAS BEEN INTERESTED IN POLITICS SINCE AN EARLY AGE. He was elected to the Albert Legislature in 1997 and took over the leadership of the Alberta New Democrats in 2000.

"I find when I've finished reading a book I feel humbled about how we live but I also feel extremely enriched."

"I grew up in a household where reading was a daily affair. My mum hadn't had the opportunity to go to school so she didn't read. My dad was very engaged in politics so there were lots of guests to entertain. He was an avid reader and a rare example, in India in the late '30s, of someone who had his own library. He also had the material means to take time to read.

I've always loved reading. I've been an academic all my life and reading has been an imperative but also a joy. Since I left academia it's been a struggle to read widely and broadly. I've given myself the luxury of reading three or four good novels at Christmas and I choose from ones which have attracted lots of attention.

I find reading of fiction exceedingly enjoyable. Through fiction I have the opportunity to partake in the experience of other people. Fiction writers bring us situations, dilemmas, paradoxes that we as human beings face, and I find that absolutely amazingly enjoyable and also liberating. We get entrapped in the daily routines, but reading takes us beyond our own experience. It's a very powerful way of doing this. I find when I've finished reading a book I feel humbled about how we live but I also feel extremely enriched. I'm not religious in the traditional sense, but there is something almost to the level of spirituality about reading because you are engaged on a much higher level in the experience of living vicariously. It humanizes you. It leads to your personal and emotional growth. It gives you an opportunity to be far more understanding, far more tolerant, and in some ways more celebratory. You're amazed at what writers can imagine. I've developed a very profound respect for people who write fiction.

For someone like me who has been in politics for eight years there are pressures, tensions, time constraints—so reading is not only an escape but also a relaxation. I find it intellectually very relaxing. I go home with a mind full of ideas, things that didn't happen, what to do tomorrow. I need to disengage in order to recharge my batteries and reading is an opportunity to withdraw from the pressures of politics. It transports me to a very different milieu. There's a physiological fatigue that sets in when you're doing intellectual work. I find reading in that sense sort of like massage therapy." 🍎

Reading List

Salt: A World History – Mark Kurlansky

The Story Behind Alberta Names: How Cities, Towns, Villages and Hamlets got Their Names – Harry Max Sanders

The Polished Hoe – Austin Clarke

Empire: A Novel – Gore Vidal

A Fine Balance – Rohinton Mistry

Rogue Nation: The America the Rest of the World Knows – Peter Scowen

Alberta Politics Uncouvered: Taking Back Our Province – Mark Lisac

"It's difficult to continue reading if something doesn't engage you."

*"Half the experience of a
book is turning the pages,
the way it smells and sounds."*

Leah Kasinsky

LEAH IS A SIXTEEN-YEAR-OLD STUDENT IN GRADE 11. She lives with her mom and dad in cooperative housing in Vancouver. Last year she spent four months living in Barcelona, Spain.

"I didn't always read well. Then in Grade 4 I started with Nancy Drew and that just led me on and on. I read a lot now, probably two or three books a month. My most recent book was *Lullaby* by Chuck Palahniuk. He's the best trashy novel writer I've ever read. I'm also reading *Steppenwolf* by Herman Hesse and I'm trying to get through *Buddha* by Karen Armstrong because I'm going to see the Dali Lama when he comes here. When I was in Spain I read up about the history and it made it a lot more interesting.

I mostly get books from the public library. I usually go with something in mind. I like old-fashioned covers. I don't like new paperbacks. I like a good thick book that looks like it is a hundred years old. That's why I could never read books on line. There's something rustic about reading. I like the texture of the pages, the way it feels in your hands. Half the experience of a book is turning the pages, the way it smells and sounds. I give away most of my books now but later I'd love to have a collection of Canadian authors.

I read in bed, in the park, on the balcony, on the bus, in school, in class. *(Laughs.)* It depends on the teacher whether they care or not. If they don't care I'll stop paying attention and start reading. If they do care, sometimes you can have the textbook open and put the book inside. I get pretty good grades—maybe it affects my grades a bit but I think it's worth it. I always carry a book around with me, right now it's Herman Hesse in my lovely cloth cover. I use the library receipt as a bookmark.

I like a really good narrative. I like to identify with the characters. I like it when they are unpredictable—when you don't know what's going to happen next, when you can't guess the ending. I love stories that are out of the ordinary but still feel like they could actually happen, like the book *Wind-up Bird Chronicle*. It's all way out of the blue, everything that happens is unexpected but at the same time it's weird, it's magic—but the author convinces you it could have actually happened. That's what gets me excited about a book." ❧

"I mostly get books from the public library. I usually go with something in mind. I like old-fashioned covers. I don't like new paperbacks. I like a good thick book that looks like it is a hundred years old."

The Learning Centre Book Club

THIS BOOK CLUB GETS TOGETHER EVERY WEEK AT THE BOYLE STREET CO-OP. The members of the group want to improve their reading and comprehension skills. "We're like a family," says James, "we all help each other." Lillian Gallant, the coordinator of the group, nods in agreement, "We read from the heart," she adds.

"I enjoy running this group because a lot of students are shy to read to other people. But here the students feel very comfortable and I feel comfortable, because if I don't know a word there's always a student who knows it."

David: This is my first time in a group. I enjoy reading, and when you're in a group you get to know the others. And I enjoy having their company because they are reading as well.

James: It's inspiring and enjoyable. It helps you get up to a higher level of reading because a lot of people have trouble reading—and the more you read, the better you get. If I get stuck they'll help me and I'll help them, and you get all this feedback. I'm getting better about reading. My reading used to be too low.

Lillian: I enjoy running this group because a lot of students are shy to read to other people. But here the students feel very comfortable and I feel comfortable, because if I don't know a word there's always a student who knows it. We read aloud together and then we talk about the story. I like the Native books because they're down to earth and the group here really enjoys them. The true stories inspire you. Everybody here helps each other. When they come in they feel good about themselves, and when they leave they feel good about themselves.

Barbara: I like to be in a group because then I learn more about the book and I can learn to read better. I stumble many times to read and Cindy helps me with the big words. She's my inspiration.

Cindy: It's helped me with reading. When I first came here I used to just read a mile a minute to get through the paragraph and get out of reading. Now I'm more comfortable. With this group I've slowed down and I understand better.

Oulinda: I really enjoy reading books. When I was a child I never read books. Sometimes the words are very hard for me but Lillian or Cindy helps me. I like to read anything because reading is very important. ❧

"We read from the heart"

"*I find that books can be your best teachers or best friends.*" ❧

Mary Tong

MARY CAME TO CANADA FROM HONG KONG WHEN SHE WAS EIGHTEEN. She now works in municipal government. When her husband died four years ago she had to learn how to cope by herself as he had managed all aspects of their life together.

"I've been reading non-stop, sometimes two or three books at the same time. Not because I find one boring but because my mind is very open to receiving information. At this point in my life I can appreciate my freedom. I have a lot of freedom and that spills over to my reading.

I guess the reason I got into all those personal growth books is because I needed to grow. I had come to a standstill. And because of life changes, all of a sudden I needed to grow in another direction.

When I moved into my condo, that change spilled over into every aspect of my life. I started to clear out my stuff. I got rid of my desk, just to keep life simple I donated books to the library. All I need is the book I'm reading. I don't need a bookcase. I keep about ten books in a basket for as long as I want and then I put them in the basement. Before, when I kept lots of books, it was the sight of the books that made me happy but I found I don't need that. I'm enjoying my reading just the same. It seems that I need less external things.

I write in books, especially in these last few years—responding to the books, notes to myself, or thoughts. It's a private thing. I realize that I will never go back to read them because it's an on-going process—it serves a purpose. But I find I'm outgrowing that. I said to myself that I'm not going to write on this book because I might want to lend it to someone.

Right now I'm going through a stage when I want to focus on uplifting things. But when books make me sad they don't make me unhappy. Because it's a portrayal of truth in life. I feel that the book is talking to me. I find that books can be your best teachers or best friends.

Time doesn't go slowly when I read—it's quality time for me. I look forward to it. I need to control myself—sometimes I can get absorbed with reading and it can cut into my sleeping time." 🍎

"All I need is the book I'm reading. I don't need a bookcase. I keep about ten books in a basket for as long as I want and then I put them in the basement."

Laurie Greenwood

LAURIE IS WELL KNOWN IN EDMONTON FOR HER INSIGHTFUL BOOK REVIEWS AND FOR HER MARVELLOUS BOOKSTORE. Her passion for books influences everything she does, from earning a living to her hobbies of reading, gardening, and cooking. She reckons she's lucky to own a bookstore as it supports her main habit of collecting books.

 ne of the things I love most about reading is that one book leads to another and another. You might read a great novel that takes place in Burma and the next thing you know you're in the history section looking for books on Burma—that may lead you to Bernard Lewis or Karen Armstrong on religion. That's just so cool!

I often say that working here at night alone, I never feel alone—all the characters are here in my mind. It's like this bookstore is always full of activity. All my friends are here with me.

I really do believe that you can't tell a book by its cover. Some books are gorgeous works of art and to most people it is important what a book looks like. Some people are really picky—they look at every page, there can't be a dent. And there are other people who couldn't care less. A lot of people smell books! I don't. But they love the smell of a fresh book.

For real book lovers like myself, buying books is as important as a fine dinner or buying a piece of art. It's a very aesthetic, personal, and necessary thing. Is it indulgent? Yes, but it's a very necessary indulgence.

"For real book lovers like myself, buying books is as important as a fine dinner or buying a piece of art."

I have a huge library at home with a lot of signed books. One of the things I love about being a bookseller is that I've met some of my favourite authors. I'm an author groupie. Sometimes my kids will go in and grab a book and I'll go, 'Wait a minute. Stop! It's my first edition. You can't read that. Go to the store and get your own.' *(Laughs.)* I'm kind of bad that way.

I have a horrible addiction to bookstores. I go all the time. I go out with my friend, who's a collector. We go to second hand bookstores, garage sales, and auctions. I go to bookstores everywhere I go except airport bookstores—I find those extremely boring. It's more personal interest than business. I just love books."

"I never feel alone— all the characters are here in my mind."

Reading List

One Hundred Years of Solitude -
Gabriel Garcia Marquez

A Prayer for Owen Meany -
John Irving

The Colony of Unrequited Dreams -
Wayne Johnston

No Great Mischief -
Alistair MacLeod

"*I like the feeling of having lots of information around me.*"

Roy James

ROY WAS BORN IN JAMAICA TO AN INDIAN FATHER AND AN ENGLISH
MOTHER. He lives on a disability pension and spends most of his free time doing volunteer
work and entering contests. Though his father was a doctor from India and his mother was
English, Roy has always felt more Jamaican. He says, "I identify with the happy-go-lucky love
of nature that is typical of Jamaicans."

"I started reading in my twenties. I remember reading all of James
Michener's books. I like adventure and descriptions of life and
people and his great stories. I've read *The Drifters* quite a few times.
I read mostly for enjoyment, occasionally for information. I
enjoy travel magazines and read those all the time. I like *Reader's Digest* because it
covers a variety of topics, short and long. I like to increase my vocabulary. I'm
interested in health and I read all the health magazines like *Alive*. And I always
read the newspaper from top to bottom. If I go away I get a friend to save me all
the copies of the newspaper. If something in the newspaper appeals to me I'll go
and do further reading.

I like to enter contests and that involves a lot of looking around. At first I
never won anything but one year I won a trip to California and a trip to Barbados
and then I was sold on entering contests. If they ask for special information,
I often have to go to the library and do research. When I go on a trip, I always
read travel books—if I don't have time beforehand, I'll do it on the plane.

I pick up a lot of free reading material and I use the library. I save up a lot
of *Reader's Digest* for when I go on holiday. I enjoy a really good magazine—it's a
definite treat.

I always read part of the newspaper in the morning and the other part when
I'm eating at night. I have a lot of books and papers in my apartment. I like the
feeling of having lots of information around me." 🐚

*"If I go away I get a friend
to save me all the copies of
the newspaper. If something
in the newspaper appeals
to me I'll go and do
further reading."*

Eva Radford

EVA WAS BORN IN NEW MEXICO AND GREW UP SPEAKING SPANISH AND ENGLISH. Many years ago she made her way to Edmonton where she works as a freelance editor. A recent visitor to her house said, "It looks as if you've been burgled but they didn't take anything." Eva admits that piles of books clutter almost all the surfaces in her home but that's the way she likes it.

"I need at least one half an hour to read something every day. I guess it's a basic need and if it's not met I don't feel happy."

"People are often amazed at the amount of books we have. My husband Tom has more books than I do because he will not throw anything out. His little office had shelves running up and down the room so you had aisles with bookshelves and some of those books were two deep. I was getting worried about the floor collapsing beneath the weight. So when we built the addition we had the carpenter make sure that the floor was sturdy. When Tom's mother died we inherited her books. I've kept them all. So it's a library, but only Tom and I know where things are. We both have piles to read. Our house is full of books and stuff—we even have more dogs than we should, and two cats. I can't imagine living in a house without books and pets. To me it would be a very boring empty place. I've been in houses like that and they give me a feeling of anxiety.

I'm an introvert and I think introverts read more. People who like quiet times can get through a lot of books. I need at least one half an hour to read something every day. I guess it's a basic need and if it's not met I don't feel happy. I always have several books going. I've been that way since I was a kid—a book in every room and a book in the purse. It's harder to keep track of them the older you get. I balance out the mysteries with heavier things—a diet of too much of the light stuff makes me feel too fluffy.

I love making a discovery—like the Ursula Bentley book I just read. I always read the *Globe and Mail* obituaries and I saw this photo of a heavy-set woman dressed in a black fur coat standing in a field at night and there's this funny flash around her. The person who wrote the obit was obviously very impressed by her. I've read a lot of English women novelists so I was surprised I'd never heard of her. I found one large print novel of hers at the library. I checked it out (the large print was easy to read—that was a discovery) and I found that she's incredibly funny and quirky. It was like discovering a new Barbara Pym." 🥀

"*I can't imagine living in a house without books and pets.*" ✤

Reading List

Any of Barbara Pym's novels

Mrs. Dalloway - Virgina Woolf

Shakespeare's Face - Stephanie Nolen

A Nest of Singing Birds - Susan Charlotte Haley

"Books are my window to a lot of stuff outside of me." ❧

Reading List

Stones from the River, and *Floating in my Mother's Palm* – Ursula Hegi

Swann, *The Republic of Love*, and *Larry's Party* – Carol Shields

Paula – Isabel Allende

For Children

The Gruffalo, and *Monkey Puzzle* – Julia Donaldson and Axel Scheffler

The Stella Series – Mary-Louise Gay

The Olivia Series – Ian Falconer

Lara Minja

LARA GREW UP IN SASKATCHEWAN ALWAYS KNOWING SHE WANTED TO
SEE MORE OF THE WORLD. "Books were my introduction to other cultures and languages,"
she says. While at university she went on an exchange trip to Germany. This experience opened
her eyes to a wider world. She now runs a graphic design company with her husband, Matthias.

"I was always a really shy kid and books were my companion. In some ways I think that books can sometimes satisfy me more than other people can. Also I really enjoy being by myself, and reading is something that you can always do.

As a new parent I thought I have to bond with my child and I don't know how to, so why don't I get her used to my voice. I started reading to her. I also wanted to instill that love of reading, to get her to listen to sounds of language. Her father is German so she hears two languages.

I love designing books because they are so worthwhile to have around. A lot of stuff we design is so temporary—brochures or posters—but a book stays around and people tend to cherish them. You can put your heart and soul into designing a book and it makes all the difference for a reader.

How a book feels and looks is important. That's what grabs my attention on the shelf. If it's nicely designed inside I feel better reading it. I guess there's a sensuousness about books. They become part of your collection, like old friends, it's hard to give them up.

Most of the friends I have are good readers. I don't know if we talk about books a lot but I think it means we're the same kind of people." ❦

*"You can put your heart
and soul into designing a
book and it makes all the
difference for a reader."*

Gary Boucher

His family trace their roots back to Louis Riel and have lived in Alberta for over two hundred years.

"There's a sense of reward knowing that I can read effectively—the gift of reading has enhanced my life and presented a lot of different opportunities."

"Reading as a child was tough for me because we didn't have electricity or a lot of light in some of the log homes we lived in. So you had to read during daylight hours, sometimes with the light from a coal oil lamp.

As a teenager I really got interested in reading Zane Gray and Louis L'Amour. I liked the description, the interactions between people, the choice of words. I was somewhat of a loner growing up and the characters in those novels were always alone—the rough western type. They'd travel, meet new people, get involved in adventures and conflicts which all had different outcomes. It would always be in a live action type of setting—a mountainside or a prairie—with descriptions of what it was like sitting beside an open fire with just a horse for company, listening to the sounds in the air, getting up at 3:30 to start the day, what the heat was like, the thirst, and living on hard tack and very little food— I could become a part of that story. I would have liked to have lived like that, and still today one of my dreams is to move back to the country, preferably the foothills, and have a log cabin.

Reading expands my ability to think and enhances the ability to speak. There's a sense of reward knowing that I can read effectively—the gift of reading has enhanced my life and presented a lot of different opportunities. My parents couldn't read. My father always said, 'Go to school, work hard, you're going to need your education.' And he was right. Although he'd never gone to school a day in his life and wasn't able to read his name. My mother was taken out of school in Grade 2 to go and live in the wilderness with her parents.

My first language was Cree. I failed Grade 1 because I couldn't speak English. I dropped out of school in Grade 10, but the fact that I had developed a love of reading when I was younger provided me with the foundation to do more." 🍎

Reading List

The Celestine Prophecy - James Redfield

Atlas Shrugged - Ayn Rand

Comstock Lode - Louis L'Amour

1984 - George Orwell

One Day in the Life of Ivan Denisovich - Alexander Solzhenitsyn

Mad Trapper - Rudy Wiebe

"Reading stimulates my creativity."

*"Reading to me is
solace and comfort."*

Christine Brophy

CHRISTINE LIVES WITH HER FAMILY IN VANCOUVER WHERE SHE HAS HER OWN ACCOUNTING BUSINESS. Every morning she rounds up Katie and Trixie, her two beagles, and heads to the beach.

"I get up at six and run around getting stuff organized for the kids and then I come here [Kitsilano Beach] to do tai chi. I take a book with me and read on the way down and then I take my dogs for a walk and read and walk. It's efficient with my time. *(Laughs.)*

If I take a break in the afternoon, I'll walk and read—I've become very inventive because it gets dark early in the winter, so I have a flashlight set around my neck. I read in the rain, so sometimes I have the flashlight and an umbrella and I wrap my book in plastic and read through the plastic—I'm that hooked on books! It's funny because people think I can't see around me when I'm walking, so they play games and try to bump into me but I have very good peripheral vision. I never trip or fall even when I go on trails. I don't even think about it—I get totally lost in my book and I enjoy it. The dogs are wonderful—they stay right with me even when they are off leash. I can usually get through a thousand pages a week just walking to and from places. I hate it when I finish a book in the middle of a walk. Sometimes if it's near the end, I'll leave it at home and take another book with me.

Reading to me is solace and comfort. When I was younger—I was one of those ugly duckling kids—I spent a lot of time on my own and reading was a great comfort for me. It relaxes me. I work with engineers and architects setting up systems, so reading is an escape from that. It's like tai chi, it has that meditative aspect to it. I don't think about anything else when I'm reading and it doesn't demand anything from me. I can do it at my own pace and I can choose whatever I want to read." 🦉

"The dogs are wonderful—they stay right with me even when they are off leash. I can usually get through a thousand pages a week just walking to and from places."

The Friends' Book Club

THIS GROUP OF WOMEN HAS BEEN MEETING REGULARLY FOR EIGHT YEARS. They got to know each other through their involvement in their children's school program. Eventually they decided they wanted to connect to one another on a different level, so they started a reading group. "Our rule at the beginning was that we were not allowed to talk about the school our kids attended," says Marce, "and whoever picks the book makes the dessert, which we attempt to relate to something in the book."

"I know my reading is way richer because of the people here. They also make me more accountable for what I read."

Heather: We take it in turn to choose books. I like books that are rich in language and in the amount of information that's included in the story.

Debbie: Heather brings a lot of culture to our group. I feel a little folksy next to her. *(Everyone laughs.)* Different books appeal to each of us. I know my reading is way richer because of the people here. They also make me more accountable for what I read. When I'm looking for a book, a little bit of me wants to wow them with my choice. Some of these people can take risks and not even read the book before they suggest it—I could never risk that.

Val: Sometimes, for myself, I just read for escapism so I'm not reading to better myself or extend my social circle or experiences. I'll read sci-fiction or fantasy that doesn't have any layers. Being in the club has expanded the types of books I read so my reading experience is more diverse. I wouldn't want to go any way from that now. It's taught me to step outside my comfort zone and look for books that are more interesting.

Marce: I like the insight that other people bring to literature. I read in one way and I like certain things. Then, when we sit down to discuss a book I find that other people bring things I haven't thought about. I learn a lot about the other people in the group by the books they choose and by the passion that they have for the books they've chosen.

Val: When I'm reading a book for myself, I just read it for pleasure. When I'm reading a book that's going to be discussed, I definitely look at the layers—I look for symbolism, allegorical content, all that stuff. I definitely get more out of the books I read for the book club because of that.

Left to right: Philomena Martens, Val Crockett, Marce Merrill, Deborah Larson, Heather Pick.

Debbie: It's a little bit intimate sharing something that you've enjoyed. You can feel a little disappointed if they don't have the same experience as you had. It's like you've let them down or they've let you down.

Marce: There are some books that I know connect with me deeply and so when we discuss them I feel that I'm letting everyone know this is really me and that's okay.

Debbie: There's a revealing of our souls in this group and it feels very safe. 🍎

Reading List

The Time Traveler's Wife –
Audrey Niffenegger

Lambs of God – Marele Day

What the Body Remembers –
Shauna Singh

The Cunning Man – Robertson Davies

Fortunes Rocks – Anita Shreve

Crow Lake – Mary Lawson

The Red Tent – Anita Diamant

Shipping News – Annie Proulx

Tulip Fever – Deborah Moggach

"Sometimes I incorporate the things I've read into my dreams." ❧

Reading List

The Egg and I – Betty MacDonald

Village of the Small Houses –
Ian Ferguson

The Hacienda –
Lisa St. Aubin de Teran

White Cargo – Felicity Kendal

And When Did You Last see Your Father? – Blake Morrison

Home Truths: A Life Around My Father – Penny Junor

Marjorie Helliwell

Marjorie doesn't hesitate. "Reading is my greatest joy," she says, "and my favourite place is the library." Marjorie left the British Isles in her late forties to come to Canada with her husband and teenage son. She is now seventy-eight and is still a busy homemaker and part-time painter and potter.

"*R*eading was my only form of relaxation for many years. My husband travelled for his work and we didn't have television. It was like a treat to myself to think, I'll do some food shopping and then I'll call in at the library.

When my son was young I could take the pram into the library but I'd get palpitations in case he'd start crying. In those days there were signs all over the library, 'Silence' and 'No talking'. So I'd buy a loaf of bread and give it to him. I'd come out with books and mutilated loaves of bread—but it was worth it.

Then I couldn't wait to get home, clear off the supper things, put the children to bed, and read.

I never buy books because once I've read a book I don't want to read it again. Now I have three libraries less than ten minutes away, so wherever I'm doing some shopping I'll call in at the library. I don't get fines very often but if it's only a couple of dollars I think it's well worth it for the amount of reading I do. I read in bed every night. Sometimes I incorporate the things I've read into my dreams. I read at breakfast—maybe one or two chapters—and in the bath, and at lunchtime, and at dinnertime if I'm by myself. I'm very rarely at home in the afternoon, but if I am and I don't have anything to do, I'll read. If I don't have anything to read I'll go to the library again as soon as I can.

I feel excited and exhilarated when I get a book. Now that I'm older I prefer biographies. Other people's lives fascinate me. I'm nosey—not to be malicious but inquisitive. And I like books that make me laugh. I like true murder mysteries as well—can't tell you why. I used to like reading about war escapes and women spies. My heart would sometimes pound up and down reading those stories. I wouldn't want to do that. I'm not a daredevil, I know my limitations.

My mother loved reading but when I took her to the library she'd just sit in the chair. And I'd say, 'What are you doing that for?' And she'd say, 'I'm waiting for you to get me some books,' which I thought was really funny because I wouldn't want anyone to choose books for me."

"Now that I'm older I prefer biographies. Other people's lives fascinate me. I'm nosey—not to be malicious but inquisitive."

JULIE WAS BORN IN NEW BRUNSWICK BUT NOW LIVES IN THE
GASPEREAU VALLEY IN NOVA SCOTIA. Her passion is spinning and weaving
and she works in a lovely fibre store ideally situated in a converted barn on a sheep farm.

"When I first started weaving I couldn't find anyone to help so I was learning from books. I got Deborah Chandler's *Learning to Weave* and I went step by step. The first time I warped a loom it was by myself using that book. I'd just seen it done before, and I made it happen because I was desperate. So I think books and magazines are an integral part of learning this craft because the communities are so isolated. There're more knitters than spinners and weavers, so you rely on the publications to connect you with other people. Newsletters are really important as well, and as much as technology is a curse it's also useful.

When choosing a pattern book, some people are very technical and they want just the facts. For me, I want to hear about how the author got into knitting and why she designed this pattern, how she used plants from their garden to dye wool, and the reasons why she uses the colours. I love to get those personal insights into why authors are doing what they doing. It makes the piece more special.

There's a book called *Knit Lit*, which is little stories from knitters all across North America. People tell stories about how they came to do whatever project they're doing. It's very successful and now they've come out with a second edition.

I use books for inspiration in every part of my life. I don't cook a lot but I have a collection of over one hundred cookbooks and I love the ones that have stories and pictures in them and are from special places. I'm not a gardener but I have gardening books—I love to look at flowers and plants. Our house is swamped with books but I did a culling recently and now I have a $70 credit at the used bookstore." 🦉

"I love to get those personal insights into why authors are doing what they doing. It makes the piece more special."

"I use books for inspiration in every part of my life." ❖

Reading List

Why Christianity Must Change or Die: A Bishop Speaks to Believers in Exile - John Shelby Spong

A History of God: The 4,000-Year Quest of Judaism, Christianity and Islam - Karen Armstrong

The Battle for God - Karen Armstrong

Why People Believe Weird Things: Pseudoscience, Superstition and other Confusions of Our Time - Michael Shermer

"When I read, time is not important to me." ❧

Edson Phipps

EDSON WAS BORN IN TRINIDAD BUT MOVED TO MONTREAL WHEN HE
WAS TWELVE. He's worked as a preacher, teacher, and nurse. Recently he owned a nursing
home for seniors but sold it to spend more time on his own projects. He has plans to build a
house in Florida.

"I read for information. My reading is limited to that right now, simply because of my interests—because of the religious journey I'm on. There's so much to uncover.

When I read, time is not important to me. Time with the author becomes the essence of why I'm there. That determines the amount of time I read. I lock myself in the little world and when I get out it's time to get something else done, but I never rush that time with the author.

I love reading in the morning—it's relaxing. I'm an early riser; I get up at 4:30 to 5 every morning. I read out loud. That's from my preaching—I like to hear the expression of a particular thought. I think it does help me with comprehension as well. If I read at any other time I would tend to fall asleep, so that's another reason why I tend to read out loud.

I read at my desk downstairs. I have to be sitting up—slouching does not do it—and always with a pen in my hand. I write in my books. I underline and I write comments. I'm interacting with the author. There are times when I disagree with what the author is saying and I'll put a question mark. But I would not turn the author away—I'm still finding out information and he or she may have a point of view I haven't seen and I need to interact with that. A question mark may indicate that I need to go back and look at that again.

The kind of emotion I experience when I read some of these authors is relief. Someone is saying something that I've been struggling with or somebody has opened up a window for me to peek in. I'm never angry with an author—more relief and joy that I'm not alone in my thoughts, because when I left the traditional teachings of the church it was like stepping into this wilderness. I have books that will travel with me where ever I go because they represent that aspect of my life when I began making sense of what my world is all about—when a huge light came on for me." 🍎

"I love reading in the morning—it's relaxing. I'm an early riser; I get up at 4:30 to 5 every morning. I read out loud."

Elly Nicolay

ELLY GRADUATED FROM UNIVERSITY A YEAR AGO WITH A DEGREE IN ANTHROPOLOGY. She is now working full time but admits she's still searching for the ideal career. She has just moved from her parents' house to her first apartment. She loves to practice aikido and tai chi and she knows exactly what she likes to read.

"My fascination with people leads me to choose books that are more about character development than action. I'd rather get to know the characters.

My mom reads as much as I do but she reads romance novels and I abhor romance novels. They can get me angry—the male character giving the female character permission to go and get a career—and I'm thinking, You don't need his permission! I asked my mom why she reads those kind of books and she said, 'It's because they don't require me to think.' But I like books that require me to think. In fact I'm drawn to them, especially if they make me think a little differently than I did before.

I find reading can be escapist. If I'm enjoying it I get absorbed. For instance, I hate watching a movie based on a book before I read the book because it just totally ruins it. When I read a book I have my own mental image of what the characters look like and what the scenery looks like. The movie is someone else's interpretation and it doesn't always mesh with mine. Then I find I'm influenced by the movie when I'm reading the book afterwards, and I'd much rather make my own images.

I love it when I get so into a book that it's sad when it ends. That's it—I'll never go there again. I have to get over it. I couldn't read the same book over and over again. I just get absorbed in another book." 🍎

"I like books that require me to think. In fact I'm drawn to them, especially if they make me think a little differently than I did before."

"I love it when I get so into a book that it's sad when it ends." ❧

"*I'm a very passionate person and I like it when books or people affect me—when something touches my soul.*" ❧

Reading List

The Case for Israel - Alan Dershowitz

Good Solider Schweik - Jaroslav Hasek

The Master and Margarita - Mikhail Bulgakov

Izabella Orzelski Konikowski

IZABELLA IS A PORTRAIT ARTIST WHO GREW UP IN POLAND. She and her husband are currently working on a series of portraits called "Unsung Heroines". "Literature is an inseparable part of my life," says Izabella, who confesses to a great passion for all the arts as well as history and politics.

"It doesn't matter how busy I am, I always have to find a place—at least half an hour for myself when I can detach from the world with a good book which takes me into my own world."

"My mother was a teacher, she told us stories and we always had lots of books at home. My dad was like a god to me and I wanted to show him that I appreciated the same things so I started picking out history books. I was bringing heavy volumes from the library. There was a limit, so I took extra cards from my mom and my father. That's when my love for history and politics began.

There was a very good magazine in Poland made up of political articles taken from around the world. Of course it was censored but it still was interesting. There was a limited number each town could get, so you had to have a good relationship with the person who was selling it. I was still a little girl but I made this connection with the gentleman and because he appreciated that I had such an interest he always left it for me on the side. One day I came and he had died and I was so sad—not only that he died but that I lost my magazine.

When I was taking a history class here I was also reading one of Gabriel Marquez's books and I wasn't prepared for the quiz. I went to the professor and said, 'I'm not prepared because I was reading such a great novel and you should read it too. I'm sorry. Give me another chance.' And he did. That was nice of him. I couldn't stop reading it because it was so beautiful. It moved me so much, I was crying, I was laughing. It was amazing. I could even smell things.

I become myself when I read like that. I'm a very passionate person and I like it when books or people affect me. When something touches my soul, I grow as a person and I'm a better person—and that's the purpose of any kind of art. It has to make us better people—make us more sensitive. That's why you have to read.

Computers give you easy access to the news and other things but books create intimacy, which we all need. It doesn't matter how busy I am, I always have to find a place—at least half an hour for myself when I can detach from the world with a good book which takes me into my own world." 🍎

RICHARD WAS BORN IN CAPE BRETON. He cleaned carpets for twelve years but always knew he'd do something else. Seven years ago he got the chance to buy a comic book store and jumped at it. He admits that sometimes it's tough to make a living but says, "Everybody should combine something they love with a business."

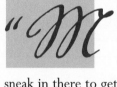

y first memory of reading was the daily funnies in the paper—"The Wizard of Id" or "Charlie Brown". When we were small we weren't supposed to go in my parents' bedroom where my father had a bookcase. I was seven and I used to sneak in there to get a book. If I had asked, I'm sure they would have said, 'Go ahead.' But it was the idea that I wasn't supposed to go in the bedroom that made it appealing. I found *The Complete Peanuts*. When I discovered it I used to slip inside the bedroom, read a few pages, and put the book back and take off. Comic strips were my first love.

It's always easier to pick up a comic book and read it because it doesn't require the same sort of attention that a novel does.

There are three aspects to reading a comic book. You can look at the visuals and just enjoy the art. You can read through the balloons and enjoy the story. And then you can compare what the words are saying to the pictures and get another level of detail towards the story.

"It's always easier to pick up a comic book and read it because it doesn't require the same sort of attention that a novel does."

When the owner of this store was trying to sell it because he saw the decline of the comic book, I bought the business from him. Most people would think, Isn't that the wrong time to buy the business? But for me that's when it became more interesting because the people who are searching for comics now are people who really enjoy them, not people who are going to bag them and board them and put them in a box and twenty years from now try to make a big profit. Those kind of collectors have gone so I don't have to deal with that mentality." 🦉

"Comic strips were

my first love." ❧

Reading List

A Heartbreaking Work of Staggering Genius - David Eggers

The Conversations: Walter Murch and the Art of Editing - Michael Ondaatje

The Hippopotamus - Stephen Fry

Pattern Recognition - William Gibson

Into Thin Air - Jon Krakauer

Fall On Your Knees - Ann-Marie MacDonald

"I like the feeling of having books that I haven't read around me."

Mieko Ouchi

MIEKO GREW UP IN CALGARY. After a brief flirtation with science at university she switched to the arts. She is now an award-winning actor, director, and playwright. She has filled her small house with books, which she admits is the main thing she misses when she's on the road.

"My mother tells a story about me when I was three. I was obsessed with books and I desperately wanted to read. One of my favourite books was *The Flopsy Bunnies* by Beatrice Potter. I would make my mom read it to me over and over again until I had memorized it, including when to turn the pages. My party trick was to read the book to people, including the line, 'It made them feel soporific'—it always terrified people to see this three-year-old talking about feeling soporific.

To my parents' horror I started reading Nancy Drew books in elementary school. My mother is a feminist and wasn't too thrilled that I was reading Nancy Drew. She kept reminding me that girls don't need their boyfriends to help them on their adventure. But I really liked them and so did my two best friends, so we would go to each other's houses and each read a Nancy Drew from cover to cover and then we'd act out the story.

When we got to junior high my best friend, Semi Chellas, who's now a film-maker, and I decided to read every book in our school library, which was a very sad little library. We only got to 'E' because we realized there were lots of really terrible books in that library. Eventually we said we have to be a bit more selective.

From wanting to read every book in the library, I've gotten much more picky about what I do read. If I'm not enjoying it, I'll stop. I know some people who will force themselves to finish a book. I don't. Although I will read anything. I have no qualms about reading Jacqueline Susann. It doesn't have to be highbrow— just entertaining or serving some function for me.

I like the feeling of having books that I haven't read around me. It's a problem anyone who's ever moved will understand. I'm not the kind of person who can take books out of the library and have no books at home. I like to own them, write in them, and put stickies in them. I like to be able to get up at three in the morning and go into my office and get this book I'm thinking about—it's some anxiety-ridden thing. I often have books for many years before I read them." 🍎

"I know some people who will force themselves to finish a book. I don't.

GLEN RECENTLY WON A GOVERNOR GENERAL'S AWARD FOR HIS CHILDREN'S BOOK, *Stitches*. Currently he's writing a young adult book about the Ukrainian internment in Alberta in WW1. Growing up in the '50s in Ashmont, a small prairie town, he relied on books for entertainment.

"My aunt, who was like an older sister, was an avid reader and a shameless purloiner of stories. She would read to us and tell us stories and sometimes the two would fuse. I remember her telling us the story of this orphan girl going to a mansion in England and being grumpy and waking up in the night and hearing cries down the hall. I didn't realize until years later that she was telling us the story of *The Secret Garden*.

When I was about twelve, my aunt's favourite book was *Gone with the Wind*, and we grew up acting out parts of that book. I remember doing dishes over my grandmother's wood-burning cookstove and acting out the entire burning of Atlanta. My grandmother yelled out from the living room, 'Aren't you ever going to finish those dishes?' And we laughed as we debated who was going to play Scarlett and who was going to be Prissy.

I used to read into the night and I'd be yelled at to turn the light out. Then I'd wait until it seemed like my parents were asleep and I'd turn it on again, or I'd cover the heating vent with a cushion so they couldn't see the light. Sometimes I'd read all night but then I'd sleep until noon the next day if it was a holiday. I was really a voracious reader when I think about it. My grandmother used to say it looked like I had a couple of coals on my face, because I had dark circles from reading all night long.

There wasn't a library in our town—well, there was one until I was five, but it was just a bunch of donated books. There wasn't anyone to look after it so they just stored the books in a municipal building. When I was thirteen, I talked someone into letting me have those books to put them out in this municipal room. That was my first job—a volunteer librarian. I commandeered some of my friends to help me set up. We talked the janitor into giving us green paint to paint the shelves. We were so anxious to get the books onto the shelves. Then we found out that the paint wasn't quite dry and we had to wrench the books off the shelves. All of them had crusts of green paint on the bottom.

"Sometimes I'd read all night but then I'd sleep until noon the next day if it was a holiday. I was really a voracious reader when I think about it."

It was a perfect job for me. I remember spending hours choosing a book to read and taking one home called *The Miracle of the Bells*. My mother said, 'You can't read that until you're eighteen,' and I said, 'Okay.' Of course, I immediately secreted it away and starting reading it, but it was so boring. Later I realized that she had mixed it up with Hemingway's *For Whom the Bell Tolls*. The library's books were mostly Book of the Month selections, so there were lots of steamy novels. So when other children were reading children's literature I was reading pulp fiction."

"I've always believed in the power of a book to startle you, amaze you, and make you laugh."

"I can't wait to get to the group and tell them about it and suggest that we all read it so that I can find out what everyone else thinks."❖

Reading List

The City of Joy - Dominique Lapierre

Are You Somebody? - Nuala O'Faolain

Wind, Sand and Stars - Antoine de Saint-Exupery

A Love of Reading - Robert Adams

Palace Walk - Naguib Mahfouz

The Prodigal Son - Henri Nouwen

Millwoods Library Book Club

THIS CLUB MEETS EVERY MONTH AT MILLWOODS LIBRARY. It's an informal group, and the number of people who turn up at each meeting varies. Jill Regan, at the library, helps the group by bringing in copies of books from other libraries.

Arline: I like being in a book club because you get to read a lot of different books—ones that you never would read on your own. And you get insights from the others in the group.

Havlik: When I read a book that I particularly enjoy, I can't wait to get to the group and tell them about it and suggest that we all read it so that I can find out what everyone else thinks. Sharing is a big thing.

Arline: You really can get excited about books and reading and you want to tell someone else about it. And you want to hear what they've read.

"I would say that I think more about the books than I used to when I read on my own."

Havlik: But that doesn't mean we're always in agreement.

Arline: That's true. We often have heated discussions!

Marta: I pay more attention now. I used to swallow a book and didn't think too much about it. Now, when I know that we're going to discuss certain passages, I even take some notes. I would say that I think more about the books than I used to when I read on my own.

Havlik: It creates more dialogue about the issue.

Arline: It often takes us out of the story in the book and we talk about politics or women's issues or whatever. 🍎

KEELY IS A YOGA TEACHER. She lives in Edmonton with her husband and their young son who likes to invent yoga moves. "My main purpose in reading right now is knowledge-seeking," admits Keely, "but I also love Spanish South American fiction."

"I read in bed. That's my favourite place. If I'm getting ready for a class or doing research, then I sit at my desk."

"I've started a study group. I've been thinking that books have a way of nurturing community, allowing people to share ideas. We're starting a Waldorf school and for the most part people don't have a deep understanding of that philosophy, so we've chosen a book that addresses that.

I read in bed. That's my favourite place. If I'm getting ready for a class or doing research, then I sit at my desk. My ideal reading situation would be a clean house and just a whole day without feeling that there's other things I need to do—to have the time to just sit and get absorbed by the book. If I'm really interested in something time can just vanish—like, oh my goodness, I've got things to do! *(Laughs.)* I'm not a fast reader. I really like to digest things.

I rarely, rarely write in books. I don't like to ruin it, you know. If I'm going to pass it on to someone else I don't want them to feel that if I've underlined a certain point it's necessarily important to them. And when I get a book I like to feel that I'm the first person who's ever read it.

My husband reads bits aloud to me but he's not receptive the other way around. *(Laughs.)* I don't absorb it very well. Often he'll read Aldous Huxley or Noam Chomsky, something like that, and he'll have gotten the point and he'll think that it's pertinent and I won't always get the before and after—just this blurb will come out and I'll be like, 'I don't get that' *(she laughs)* and he'll say, 'How can you not get that?' Often I'm reading beside him in bed and I'll think, hey wait a minute, I'm reading my own book.

Reading a good book is very satisfying. I feel whole and complete—a mind euphoria. Like reading a really good short story where every detail reflects the story, every thread gets tied up, and they all lead to the end and the end is satisfying. Of course I want more—but there's satisfaction in that too.

It's a way for me to see what's happening in myself. A reflection of what's going on outside and how that interplays within myself—what if I was in that situation, how would I react—those kind of things. It's a safe way to have an adventure." 🍎

"*Books have a way of nurturing community, allowing people to share ideas.*" ❧

"I like any book that

has a message in it." ❧

Long Walk to Freedom -
Nelson Mandela

Momo - Michael Ende

*Whispering Winds of Change:
Perceptions of a New World* -
Stuart Wilde

*Your Money or Your Life:
Transforming Your Relationship
with Money and Achieving
Financial Independence* - Joe
Dominguez and Vicki Robbins

The Story of B - Daniel Quinn

*The Energy of Money: A Spiritual
Guide to Financial and Personal
Fulfillment* - Maria Nemeth

Heather MacMillan

HEATHER FARMS NEAR WOLFVILLE, NOVA SCOTIA. When she and her partner bought Maple Hill Farm twenty years ago they grew fruit and vegetables, but over the years they have had to diversify in order to make a living. Now they concentrate on plants for home gardeners. It's probably no coincidence that their workers just happen to be avid readers too.

"I often pass on books to our workers and we talk about them. Right now, Sara is reading *Icelandia*. Elena is reading *Wild Swans*. Linda just read *The Four Agreements*. Michelle is reading *Free Parking*.

I like any book that has a message in it. I guess it's like trying on a pair of shoes. If it fits, it's for you. And it's the same with books. I like writers who aren't going with the flow.

I leave for my market around 4:45 a.m. and I get up and read before I leave and I take a break during the day and read. That seems to be relaxing for me. I have to read. For years, when I travelled to market I drove the truck and I was alone and the others would come behind. When people asked what I wanted for gifts I'd ask for books on tape and then I'd buy the book if I really liked it. *The Power of Now* was one book I remember. I liked it but I couldn't get into it, don't ask me why. Then my mother gave me the tape, and it's fantastic. He's from British Columbia and when he was twenty-nine he suffered from severe depression. He gave away everything and slept on park benches for two years and then came out with these books.

I grew up in a village where it was very difficult to get anything to read. I remember saying to my mother, 'Oh, there's nothing to read,' and she said, 'Read the cornflakes box.' I took up nursing, then I was asked to set up a clinic. I worked very hard and read a lot, let me tell you. I got burnt out and came to the country for a year. I always loved the land. I started doing a bit of haying for people. Allison had left her job and we just got together and got this place. You certainly don't do this for the money—you get a living." 🍎

"When people asked what I wanted for gifts I'd ask for books on tape and then I'd buy the book if I really liked it.

Michele Lee

MICHELE WAS BORN IN SINGAPORE. She came to Canada to take a business degree at the University of Alberta. She's now a full-time homemaker and mother and is expecting her second child.

"My mother was a school librarian so she encouraged us to read. She would take us with her when she bought books and we could choose the books we liked for the school. I have three sisters and all of us started reading really young. At lunchtime there would be four of us with a book in front of us as we ate our lunch. Finally my mum got so mad she said, 'No more reading at lunch.' Because we didn't talk to each other. We'd just read.

We read a lot of Enid Blyton—she had so many different series. When my second sister read *Lord of the Rings* we were still quite young and we used to pretend we were characters in the book. We'd always do it in the car and we'd all try to get the best characters.

I read lots of fiction, mainly the bestsellers and mysteries. I have to read every day—it's my only form of relaxation. I get very involved when I'm reading. If it's a really good book I can get so engrossed that I'll forget to do stuff—all the housework—I'll just read and read. And sometimes it's really bad at night because if it's riveting I don't want to sleep—I just want to read. I guess it's quite addictive that way.

I always talk about books with my sisters and they'll say, 'Have you read this?' That's often how I decide what to read and what's on the bestsellers list.

Reading is a break from the boring everyday things I have to do. It's so nice to just sit and read and not have to do anything. Sometimes when I run out of books to read, I'll be wandering around the house kinda bored, thinking, I have things to do but I don't want to do them. Reading is my main hobby and it's so easy for me to do it with a young child, whereas sports or something like that would be just too difficult to do." 🍎

"If it's a really good book I can get so engrossed that I'll forget to do stuff—all the housework—I'll just read and read."

"I have to read every day—it's my only form of relaxation." ❧

Reading List

To Kill a Mockingbird - Harper Lee

I am David - Anne Holm

The God of Small Things - Arundhati Roy

The Joy Luck Club - Amy Tan

Reading List

Housekeeping – Marilynne Robinson

A Good Man is Hard to Find –
Flannery O'Connor

Dream Boy – Jim Grimsley

Love Medicine – Louise Erdrich

*One Way Street and Other Writing*s –
Walter Benjamin

"Reading is selfish for me now—I do it for myself and to improve my own writing, to empower myself."

Norman Sacuta

NORM IS A WRITER WHO LIVES IN EDMONTON. He did postgraduate work in the University of Sussex in England. His latest poetry book is called *Garments of the Known*.

"I remember when I decided I didn't like to read. There was a neighbour who had a boy my age and my mother continually compared me with him. He could read a Hardy Boy in a day and it would take me two weeks. I hated the notion of reading as a competition so I stopped reading Hardy Boys. At that exact time I decided that I liked reading but I wanted to do it at my own pace. I got into the *World Almanac [and Book] of Facts* and disaster books, especially about the Titanic, which I'm still interested in.

I've never been a fast reader—it's never been because of vocabulary or an ability to understand, it's that I like to read things slowly so that I understand on some level everything that happens. It's a check on myself and my exuberance when reading—I don't like to put myself too much into the book. I want to know the author. I think you can read the personality of an author through the words he chooses so I don't want to misinterpret them.

"I've never been a fast reader—it's never been because of vocabulary or an ability to understand, it's that I like to read things slowly so that I understand on some level everything that happens."

I read almost every night before I go to bed and I'll often read early in the morning. When I read before I sleep I remember my dreams, and I'm convinced that there's a connection. I think that my dreams are more vivid because of written language. It's the language in the dreams that help me remember them.

Books are an escape. I've had situations when I had bad experiences and then what I want to do is just read—it's a way of cutting yourself off from an external reality. That's a cliché, I guess, but it's true. You can just sit with your book, unplug the phone, and just read—it's almost like a feeling of power because other people can't get hold of you and you're doing something for yourself. Reading is selfish for me now—I do it for myself and to improve my own writing, to empower myself.

Sometimes I like to read in a coffee house. I can stand the noise interrupting me better in there than in my apartment, but if someone comes up to me and interrupts my reading that bugs me. I hate that. It's like you're not doing anything, and of course you are." 🐦

PHYLLIS IS A METIS WOMAN. She co-ordinates an adult literacy program in Edmonton and loves to travel whenever possible.

"As I'm reading I put myself in the place of the character and become very involved. I think, I wouldn't do that, or, Why is she doing that?"

"*R*eading quiets my mind. When I read I'm forced to take my attention away from problems that I'm often caught up in. I do find it difficult to sit still because I'm very driven. So I enjoy reading on the stationary bike. I'm able to exercise longer and read. I'll be on the bike for an hour or sometimes two hours if there's no demand for it. Depending on the book, the hour will just flash by and I'll look down and think, Oh boy, I've only got ten minutes left!

I joined a book club because I wanted to read more. The day before the book club meeting I'd often be down at the gym on the bike ploughing through some book. So the book club has helped me read for pleasure. If I'm reading for work, then I'll often take it to the gym because I find my comprehension is much higher when I'm cycling.

Going to the gym helps me get through books that I may not like to begin with. I wanted to read *Generation X* because my children are of that generation. But I could only read a page at a time in bed, so I took it to the gym. After I got a third of the way through, I finally got engaged with the characters. Had I not taken it to the gym, I'm positive I wouldn't have read it.

As I'm reading I put myself in the place of the character and become very involved. I think, I wouldn't do that, or, Why is she doing that? I enjoy books for the insights into human nature and also my nature.

Sometimes out of the blue there will be a short statement that to me will be very profound—Margaret Atwood talking about a quilt—I don't remember which book it was—she wrote, 'One of the most dangerous places in the world is the bed because it's where we're born and it's where we die.' Then she went on to talk about the quilt and what the covering represented. I used this quote at the Centre when we were working on a quilt and we were encouraging people to see the bed from another perspective. I read for those little snippets." 🍎

"I enjoy books for the insights into human nature and also my nature." ❧

Reading List

Dombey and Son - Charles Dickens

The Picture of Dorian Gray -
Oscar Wilde

The No. 1 Ladies' Detective Agency -
Alexander McCall Smith

Tears of the Giraffe -
Alexander McCall Smith

"Time with books
is very private,
otherwise you
can't enjoy them." ❧

Reading List

Treasure Island - Robert Louis
Stevenson

All Quiet on the Western Front -
Erich Maria Remarque

Sergei Glebov

SERGEI WAS BORN IN RUSSIA. He studied and lived in Europe before settling in Canada in 1998. He is a translator and often travels back to Russia on trade missions. His love of books has resulted in a huge collection which he plans to house in a large room on the top floor of his century-old home.

"I'll organize it according to some principle—art books, children's books, military books, Russian, English, and other books. It'll be a place where I can climb in and forget the rest of the world and just be in the world of my dreams and fantasies and the world of books. I think it's going to be very private—just me and the books. Time with books is very private, otherwise you can't enjoy them. The environment will add to the pleasure of reading books and it will be my travelling room where I can travel in my mind to different times and different worlds. It's a whole world that is fascinating, sometimes frightening, sometimes thought provoking, but it's all this kaleidoscope of life, I guess, and it's all in books.

Reading *Treasure Island* takes me back in time—the pirates are gone, the kids dealing with pirates are gone, that world is gone. But I can get into that world through this book. I'm not really comparing what I would do in the situation. I find the way characters behave is outdated, they are only specific for that period and they are only justified by that time. You could say, I don't like these good moral boys who do the right things, or you could think, Well, it's all somewhere there and it's nice to touch it and experience it and see that goodness prevails. It's fascinating—you understand the naivety of it all, of course, sitting here and knowing how wise you are. But I like this kind of experience of time when you read a book like *Treasure Island*—you actually can try to live in their world. You don't judge them, you just dive in and go with them." 🍎

"The environment will add to the pleasure of reading books and it will be my travelling room where I can travel in my mind to different times and different worlds."

Sharon Laberge

SHARON ALWAYS WANTED TO HAVE A LITTLE STORE, so she took early retirement and opened a secondhand bookstore in Edmonton. "It's a gamble," she says, "but I'm really enjoying it."

"The ironic thing is that I have less time for reading now that I have a bookstore. I still really enjoy fiction, Canadian writers in particular, and nonfiction—history and politics, current events.

When books come in I want to set some aside and I have to give my head a shake. There's always too much to do. I think it's a common experience that reading can seem like a frivolous activity. A lot of people feel they should be doing the laundry or something else rather than reading. It's like a guilty pleasure, but I've gotten past that.

I like to read in the bathtub. It's funny because people are so different in terms of how they treat their books. I know people who would have a fit if they loaned me a book and knew that I was exposing it to humidity. They're the ones who take the dust jacket off and set it aside when they are reading it and then put it back on the book. I like to keep a book in fairly good shape but I don't have a fit if someone turns over the page in one of my books.

I do feel I need to read bits aloud to other people and in a way the bookstore is the way of realizing this desire to inflict books on people. When you've read a good book you want to discuss it with other people—I suppose that's the reason for book clubs or loaning a book to a friend.

I had boxes of books that hadn't been opened since our last move eight years ago. Some of my friends told me, 'I would never dream of getting rid of my books. They're part of me.' I can appreciate that. I've felt the same way about mine. But now I think that someone else could be enjoying them so quite a few of my books are in the store. But there are still quite a few at home that I wouldn't dream of parting with." 🍎

"When you've read a good book you want to discuss it with other people—I suppose that's the reason for book clubs or loaning a book to a friend."

"Reading is like
a guilty pleasure,
but I've gotten
past that." ❧

Reading List

Wilfrid Gordon McDonald Partridge -
Mem Fox

Elegy for Iris - John Bayley

A Good House - Bonnie Burnard

Siddhartha - Hermann Hesse

"When I read something,
I'll often stop and think,
How can twenty-six letters
do that to me?" ❧

Merle Harris

MERLE WAS BORN IN SOUTH AFRICA BUT SOON AFTER MOVED TO ZIMBABWE.
Her lifelong love of words and books now finds expression in her work as a storyteller and a
creator and collector of handmade books. She credits her stepfather's love of reading as having
profound influence on her.

"The Christmas I was five my stepfather gave me a *Concise Oxford
Dictionary* which appalled me. I could read the odd word, but I
wasn't a reader and here was this huge book with nothing but
words in it.

That night after I had had my bath, dad sat down with me, opened the dictionary
and said, 'Close your eyes and choose a word.' It became a ritual even after I'd
gone to boarding school. When I was home, dad and I used to choose three words
from the dictionary. He'd explain where the words came from. Then out would
come the atlas and he'd show me the countries, and we'd talk about how the
words had travelled and some of the adventures they might have had. If they
were from mythology, he'd tell me the myths. If they were words a six-year-old
shouldn't be using, my father would explain the word and say, 'It's not a word
you should use. It will upset people.' But he never turned anything down.

I think my love of reading started not long after. I twigged onto something
that has never left me. It was that everything you read revolves around twenty-six
letters. When I read something, I'll often stop and think, How can twenty-six
letters do that to me? That's the power of words! It was Jimmy, or dad as I called
him, that showed me that.

He'd read aloud things that didn't mean anything to me at all but that he
loved. He'd say, 'Listen to this.' And I'd say, 'Why?' And he'd say, 'Listen how the
words fit together.'

He never stopped me reading anything. I read *Fanny Hill* when I was nine. I'd
walk around with it and my dictionary. My dad said to me, 'Why did you choose
that book?' and I said, 'Oh, I like her name.' When I reread it in my twenties I just
about died! To think I'd walked around the mine town with people knowing that I
was reading that. But you only read what you understand.

I don't think I ever thanked him for the dictionary. I can still remember that
it smelled of leather with onionskin paper. It was well used and ended up with
rubber bands holding the cover on and I think my mum just turfed it in a spell of
getting rid of stuff."

*"When I was home, dad
and I used to choose three
words from the dictionary.
He'd explain where the
words came from. Then out
would come the atlas and
he'd show me the countries,
and we'd talk about how
the words had travelled
and some of the adventures
they might have had."*

The Fabulous Readers' Club

THIS GROUP HAS BEEN MEETING FOR THREE YEARS AT THE SPRUCEWOOD LIBRARY IN EDMONTON. Each meeting has a different theme, and the members make their own choices about what to read. They get together once a month to chat about what they've been reading and to do activities.

Naina Hinduche has been coming to the group for about three years. She loves Harry Potter books. Her mother, Diph, accompanied her to the meeting.

Naina: I like to talk to others about Harry Potter. I like reading on my own but it's fun to talk about things you really like.

Natasha Pigford joined the group because she wanted to read more books. She enjoys reading adventure books.

Natasha: I like to talk about books in a group because then I get to hear what other kids like and don't like. I like scary books the best of all.

"When I read a book by myself all the thoughts I get about the book are kept to myself. When I get to review the book then I get to share my impressions, and maybe someone else will read it."

Tamara Raynor-Cote was a member of the group for two years. Books are a big part of her family's life. Her mother and brother work in libraries and she works part-time at Sprucewood Library.

Tamara: I joined the group because of the opportunity to review books. When I read a book by myself all the thoughts I get about the book are kept to myself. When I get to review the book then I get to share my impressions, and maybe someone else will read it. When I'm thinking about my review I'm formulating new ideas and I'm learning more about the book for myself. It makes me think more about why I liked the book. It also makes me read more worthwhile books.

Maria-Elizabeth Vicente coordinates the group. She is finishing her master's in library science while working at the library.

Maria: It's very inspiring to coordinate this group because their love of reading is overwhelming. It helps to talk about books because we learn from each other. We often discover things that we wouldn't normally do if we were reading independently, because it's very much about sharing. 🐦

About the Author

SUSAN ROGERS has been the proud owner of a library card since the age of six! She has also spent a small fortune in library fines! Like most book lovers, she has personally experienced how a passion for reading can be hazardous to your wallet.

After a twenty-year career in television production, Susan made a brief foray into new media. Her credits include dramas, documentaries, and children's interactive webstories. Finally, she is writing for print, which has always been her true love.

She lives in Alberta with her husband, Reuben Kaufman and her son, Nicolas. 🍎

Reading List

The Year 1000: What Life Was Like at the Turn of the First Millennium: An Englishman's World - Robert Lacey and Danny Danziger

Touching the Void - Joe Simpson

Behind the Scenes at the Museum - Kate Atkinson

The End of Elsewhere - Taras Grescoe

Three Men in a Boat - Jerome K. Jerome